Ghassan

Ghassan 485-4760

351-5816

THIRD EDITION

ELEMENTS OF ARGUMENT

A Text and Reader

Annette T. Rottenberg

UNIVERSITY OF MASSACHUSETTS AT AMHERST

BEDFORD BOOKS OF ST. MARTIN'S PRESS
BOSTON

For Alex

For Bedford Books
Publisher: Charles H. Christensen
Associate Publisher: Joan E. Feinberg
Managing Editor: Elizabeth M. Schaaf
Developmental Editor: Stephen A. Scipione
Production Editor: Lori Chong
Copyeditor: Deborah Fogel
Text Design: Claire Seng-Niemoeller
Cover Design: Richard Emery
Cover Art: Honoré Daumier, *Lawyers and Justice* (L. Delteil No. 1343, April 24, 1845). Bequest of William P. Babcock. Courtesy, Museum of Fine Arts, Boston.

Library of Congress Catalog Card Number: 89–63931

Manufactured in the United States of America.

5   4   3   2   1

f   e   d   c   b

For information, write: St. Martin's Press, Inc.
175 Fifth Avenue, New York, NY 10010
Editorial Offices: Bedford Books *of* St. Martin's Press,
29 Winchester Street, Boston, MA 02116

ISBN: 0–312–04059–8
Instructor's Edition ISBN: 0–312–04910–2

ACKNOWLEDGMENTS

Felicia Ackerman, "Not Everybody Wants to Sign a Living Will." From the *New York Times,* October 13, 1989. Copyright © 1989 by The New York Times Company. Reprinted by permission.
Gordon Allport, "The Nature of Prejudice." From the Seventeenth Claremont Reading Conference Yearbook, 1952. Reprinted by permission.

Acknowledgments and copyrights are continued at the back of the book on pages 631–636, which constitute an extension of the copyright page.

Preface
for Instructors

PURPOSE

Argumentation as the basis of a composition course should need no defense, especially at a time of renewed pedagogical interest in critical thinking. A course in argumentation encourages practice in close analysis, use of supporting materials, and logical organization. It encompasses all the modes of development around which composition courses are often built. It teaches students to read and to listen with more than ordinary care. Not least, argument can engage the interest of students who have been indifferent or even hostile to required writing courses. Because the subject matter of argument can be found in every human activity, from the most trivial to the most elevated, both students and teachers can choose the materials that appeal to them. And those materials need not be masterpieces of the genre, as in courses based on literature; students can exercise their critical skills on flawed arguments that allow them to enjoy a well-earned superiority.

Composition courses using the materials of argument are, of course, not new. But the traditional methods of teaching argument through mastery of the formal processes of reasoning cannot account for the complexity of arguments in practice. Even more relevant to our purposes as

teachers of composition is the tenuous relationship between learning about induction and deduction, however helpful in analysis, and the actual process of student composition. E. D. Hirsch, Jr., in *The Philosophy of Composition*, wrote, "I believe, as a practical matter, that instruction in logic is a very inefficient way to give instruction in writing."[1] The challenge has been to find a method of teaching argument that assists students in defending their claims as directly and efficiently as possible, a method that reflects the way people actually go about organizing and developing claims outside the classroom.

One such method, first adapted to classroom instruction by teachers of rhetoric and speech, uses a model of argument advanced by Stephen Toulmin in *The Uses of Argument*. Toulmin was interested in producing a description of the real *process* of argument. His model was the law. "Arguments," he said, "can be compared with law-suits, and the claims we make and argue for in extra-legal contexts with claims made in the courts."[2] Toulmin's model of argument was based on three principal elements: claim, evidence, and warrant. These elements answered the questions, "What are you trying to prove?" "What have you got to go on?" "How did you get from evidence to claim?" Needless to say, Toulmin's model of argument does not guarantee a classroom of skilled arguers, but his questions about the parts of an argument and their relationship are precisely the ones that students must ask and answer in writing their own essays and analyzing those of others. They lead students naturally into the formulation and development of their claims.

My experience in supervising hundreds of teaching assistants over a number of years has shown that they also respond to the Toulmin model with enthusiasm. They appreciate its clarity and directness and the mechanism it offers for organizing a syllabus.

In this text I have adapted — and greatly simplified — some of Toulmin's concepts and terminology for freshman students. I have also introduced two elements of argument with which Toulmin is not directly concerned. Most rhetoricians consider them indispensable, however, to discussion of what actually happens in the defense or rejection of a claim. One is motivational appeals — warrants based on appeals to the needs and values of an audience, designed to evoke emotional responses. A distinction between logic and emotion may be useful as an analytical tool, but in producing or attacking arguments human beings find it difficult, if not impossible, to make such a separation. In this text, therefore, persuasion through appeals to needs and values is treated as a legitimate element in the argumentative process.

---

[1] *The Philosophy of Composition* (Chicago: University of Chicago Press, 1977), p. 142.
[2] *The Uses of Argument* (Cambridge: Cambridge University Press, 1958), p. 7.

I have also stressed the significance of audience as a practical matter. In the rhetorical or audience-centered approach to argument, to which I subscribe in this text, success is defined as acceptance of the claim by an audience. Arguers in the real world recognize intuitively that their primary goal is not to demonstrate the purity of their logic, but to win the adherence of their audiences. To gain this adherence, students need to be reminded of the necessity for establishing themselves as credible sources for their readers.

ORGANIZATION

In Part One, after an introductory overview, a chapter each is devoted to the chief elements of argument — the claims that students make in their arguments (Chapter 2), the definitions and support they must supply for their claims (Chapters 3 and 4), the warrants that underlie their arguments (Chapter 5), the language that they use (Chapter 6). Popular fallacies, as well as induction and deduction, are treated in Chapter 7; because fallacies represent errors of the reasoning process, a knowledge of induction and deduction can make clear how and why fallacies occur.

I have tried to provide examples, readings, discussion questions, and writing suggestions that are both practical and stimulating. With the exception of several student dialogues, the examples are real, not invented; they have been taken from speeches, editorial opinions, letters to the editor, advertisements, interviews, and news reports. They reflect the liveliness and complexity that invented examples often suppress.

The readings in Part One support the discussions in several important ways. First, they illustrate the elements of argument; in each chapter, one or more essays have been analyzed to emphasize the chapter's principles of argument. Second, they are drawn from current publications and cover as many different subjects as possible to convince students that argument is a pervasive force in the world they read about and live in. Third, some of the essays are obviously flawed and thus enable students to identify the kinds of weaknesses they should avoid in their own essays.

Part Two takes up the processes of writing and researching. Chapter 8 explains how to find a topic, define the issues that it embraces, organize the information, and draft and revise an argument. Chapter 9 introduces students to the business of finding sources, mostly in the library, and using them effectively in research papers. Both chapters conclude with sample student papers; the annotated student research paper in Chapter 9 uses the MLA documentation system. (The MLA system is explained along with the APA system elsewhere in the chapter.)

Part Three, "Opposing Viewpoints," exhibits arguers in action, using informal and formal language, debating head-on. The subjects —

abortion, AIDS testing, animal rights, collegiate sports reform, environmental policy, euthanasia, freedom of speech, legalizing drugs, pornography — capture headlines every day. Despite their immediacy, these subjects are likely to arouse passions and remain controversial for a long time. Whether as matters of national policy or personal choice, they call for decisions based on familiarity with their competing views.

Finally, Part Four, "Classic Arguments," reprints eight selections that have stood the tests of both time and the classroom. Drawn from the works of Plato, Jonathan Swift, Henry David Thoreau, Elizabeth Cady Stanton, Virginia Woolf, George Orwell, and Martin Luther King, Jr., they are among the arguments that teachers find invaluable in any composition course.

The editor's notes provide additional suggestions for using the book, as well as for finding and using the enormous variety of materials available in a course on argument.

I hope this text will lead students to discover not only the practical and intellectual rewards of learning how to argue but the real excitement of engaging in civilized debate as well.

NEW TO THIS EDITION

Revising a successful textbook — the publisher says that *Elements of Argument* is now the bestselling book of its kind — presents both a challenge and an opportunity. The challenge is to avoid undoing features that have been well received in the earlier edition. The opportunity is to tap into the experiences of instructors and students who have used the earlier editions and to make use of their insights to improve what needs improvement. This is how we have approached this revision, and it accounts for all that we have done, and not done, in preparing the new edition.

The principles and concerns of the book have not changed. Rather, I have included a greater breadth of material to increase the book's usefulness as a teaching tool. Instructors who requested more explanation in Part One of warrants, induction, and deduction now have more, including sample analyses of inductive and deductive arguments and discussion of the relationship of warrants to other elements of argument. Instructor interest has also led me to add several advertisements to Part One for student analysis. Part Two is a substantial revision and enlargement of the second edition's appendix on writing arguments. Library research and writing from sources are now covered in more detail, and two sample student arguments (one of them an annotated research paper) are included; also new is a section on the APA documentation system to supplement the coverage of the MLA system. In Part Three, the number of "Opposing

Viewpoints" has increased from six to nine. The five most popular topics from the second edition — AIDS Testing, Animal Rights, Collegiate Sports Reform, Euthanasia, Pornography — have been retained and brought up to date, while four new topics that should appeal strongly to students have been added: Abortion, Environmental Policy, Freedom of Speech, and Legalizing Drugs. Part Four is now a separate anthology of classic arguments, perennial favorites of instructors and students. All told, the number of selections has grown from seventy-eight in the second edition to one hundred and seventeen in the third, with a corresponding increase in the number of debatable issues (and teaching options). Taken as a whole the changes in the third edition should enhance the versatility of the book, deepen students' awareness of how pervasive argument is, and increase their ability to think critically and communicate persuasively.

This book has profited from the critiques and suggestions of Patricia Bizzell, College of the Holy Cross; Richard Fulkerson, East Texas State University; William Hayes, California State College — Stanislaus; Marcia MacLennan, Kansas Wesleyan University; Lester Faigley, University of Texas at Austin; Cheryl W. Ruggiero, Virginia Polytechnic Institute; Michael Havens, University of California at Davis; Judith Kirscht, University of Michigan; Richard Katula, University of Rhode Island; Carolyn R. Miller, North Carolina State University at Raleigh; A. Leslie Harris, Georgia State University; Richard S. Hootman, University of Iowa; Donald McQuade, University of California at Berkeley; David L. Wagner; Ron Severson, Salt Lake Community College; Paul Knoke, East Carolina University; and Robert H. Bentley, Lansing Community College. The editor's notes are the better for the contributions of Gail Stygall, Miami University of Ohio.

Many instructors helped improve the book by responding to a questionnaire. I appreciate the thoughtful consideration given by: Timothy C. Alderman, Yvonne Alexander, William Arfin, Karen Arnold, Peter Banland, Carol A. Barnes, Don Beggs, Don Black, Kathleen Black, Stanley S. Blair, Laurel Boyd, Dianne Brehmer, Alan Brown, Paul L. Brown, W. K. Buckley, Alison A. Bulsterbaum, Clarence Bussinger, Gary T. Cage, Ruth A. Cameron, Barbara R. Carlson, Gail Chapman, Roland Christian, Dr. Thomas S. Costello, Mimi Dane, Judy Davidson, Philip E. Davis, Julia Dietrich, Marcia B. Dinnech, L. Leon Duke, P. Dunsmore, Bernard Earley, Carolyn L. Engdahl, David Estes, Kristina Faber, B. R. Fein, Delia Fisher, Evelyn Flores, Donald Forand, Mary A. Fortner, Leslye Friedberg, Diane Gabbard, Frieda Gardner, Gail Garloch, E. R. Gelber-Beechler, Scott Giantralley, Michael Patrick Gillespie, Paula Gillespie, Wallace Gober, Sara Gogol, Marilyn Hagans, Linda L. Hagge, Lee T. Hamilton, Phillip J. Hanse, Susan Harland, Carolyn G. Hartz, Anne Helms, Diane Price Herndl, Heidi Hobbs, William S. Hochman, Sharon E. Hockensmith, Joyce Hooker,

Clarence Hundley, Richard Ice, Mary Griffith Jackson, Ann S. Jagoe, Katherine James, Owen Jenkins, Ruth Y. Jenkins, Janet Jubnke, E. C. Juckett, George T. Karnezis, Mary Jane Kearny, Patricia Kellogg-Dennis, Joanne Kirkland, Nancy Klug, John H. Knight, Barbara Ladd, William Levine, Cynthia Lowenthal, Marjorie Lynn, Patrick McGuire, Ray McKerrow, Pamela J. McLagan, Christina M. McVay, D'Ann Madewell, Beth Madison, Susan Maloney, Barbara A. Manrigue, Joyce Marks, Charles May, Jean-Pierre Meterean, Lisa K. Miller, Logan D. Moon, Dennis D. Moore, Dan Morgan, Curt Mortenson, Philip A. Mottola, Thomas Mullen, Michael B. Naas, Joseph Nassar, Byron Nelson, Elizabeth Nist, Dr. Mary Jean Northcutt, Thomas O'Brien, James F. O'Neil, Richard D. Olson, Lori Jo Oswald, Leland S. Person, Steve Phelan, Teresa Marie Purvis, Barbara E. Rees, Pat Regel, Charles Reinhart, Janice M. Reynolds, Douglas F. Rice, Katherine M. Rogers, Judith Klinger Rose, Cathy Rosenfeld, Robert A. Rubin, Lori Ruediger, Joseph L. Sanders, Suzette Schlapkohl, Sybil Schlesinger, Richard Schneider, Lucy Sheehey, Sallye J. Sheppeard, Sally Bishop Shigley, John Shout, Thomas Simmons, Richard Singletary, Beth Slusser, Denzell Smith, Rebecca Smith, Elissa L. Stuchlik, Judy Szaho, Andrew Tadie, R. Terhorst, Marguerite B. Thompson, Arline R. Thorn, Mary Ann Trevathan, Whitney G. Vanderwerff, Jennie VerSteeg, Linda D. Warwick, Carol Adams Watson, Roger D. Watson, Karen Webb, Raymond E. Whelan, Betty E. White, Toby Widdicombe, Heywood Williams, and Alfred Wong.

I thank the people at Bedford Books whose efforts have made the progress of the third edition a thousand times lighter for me: Jane Betz, Frank Dumais, Deborah Fogel, Ellen Kuhl, Chris Rutigliano, and Elizabeth Schaaf. Most of all I thank Charles H. Christensen, Joan E. Feinberg, Lori Chong, and the editor with whom I have worked most closely for two editions, Steve Scipione.

Brief Contents

PART TWO

Writing and Researching Arguments 251

8. *Writing an Argumentative Paper* 253
9. *Researching an Argumentative Paper* 277

PART THREE

Opposing Viewpoints 311

10. *Abortion* 315
11. *AIDS Testing* 336
12. *Animal Rights* 362
13. *Collegiate Sports Reform* 397
14. *Environmental Policy* 419
15. *Euthanasia* 443
16. *Freedom of Speech* 472
17. *Legalizing Drugs* 503
18. *Pornography* 526

PART FOUR

Classic Arguments 553

Glossary and Index of Terms 637
Index of Authors and Titles 642

Contents

Preface for Instructors   v

PART ONE

The Structure of Argument   1

1. *Introduction to Argument*   3

The Nature of Argument   3
Why Study Argument?   6
Why Write?   8
The Terms of Argument   9
The Audience   13

SAMPLE ANALYSIS

> ***The Declaration of Independence***
> *THOMAS JEFFERSON*   18

> When revolutionaries resolved to throw off their king and form their own government, they turned to the eloquent Jefferson for a defense of their audacious plan.

EXERCISES FOR REVIEW   22

2. *Claims*   24

Claims of Fact   24

SAMPLE ANALYSIS: CLAIM OF FACT

Cocaine Is Even Deadlier Than We Thought
LOUIS L. CREGLER and HERBERT MARK   **30**

Two physicians examine the frightening and potentially lethal effects of cocaine abuse.

Claims of Value   31

SAMPLE ANALYSIS: CLAIM OF VALUE

Kids in the Mall: Growing Up Controlled
WILLIAM SEVERINI KOWINSKI   **35**

A journalist evaluates the lessons teens learn in "universities of suburban materialism."

Claims of Policy   39

SAMPLE ANALYSIS: CLAIM OF POLICY

So That Nobody Has to Go to School
If They Don't Want To
ROGER SIPHER   **42**

A teacher argues that forcing unmotivated students to stay in school is a fruitless waste of energy and resources and a drag on those who truly want to learn.

READINGS FOR ANALYSIS

Homelessness in Colonial and Early America
PETER H. ROSSI   **45**

A sociologist shows that, although the homeless today arouse sympathetic attention, they were in the past treated with indifference and even "contempt, fear, and loathing."

Discriminating Tastes: The Prejudice of Personal Preferences
VICTORIA A. SACKETT   **50**

Our national tolerance of diversity has increased, writes an editor of *Public Opinion*; yet as individuals we are succumbing to a plague of petty prejudices.

In Support of Our Common Language . . .
U. S. ENGLISH   **54**

A public interest group spells out why it is important that English be the official language of the United States.

Capital Punishment — An Idea Whose Time Has Come Again
J. A. PARKER   **57**

A spokesman for a conservative African-American think tank musters evidence to show that opposition to capital punishment runs counter to our religious and legal tradition.

The Right to Bear Arms
WARREN E. BURGER   **64**

A former chief justice of the United States examines the historical roots of the Second Amendment in order to construct an appeal for gun control.

The great American forest is closer than you think
[advertisement]   68

GE: The initials of a friend [advertisement]   69

Nuclear energy can help America find a way out of our dangerous dependence on foreign oil [advertisement]   70

EXERCISES FOR REVIEW   **71**

3.   Definition   72

The Purposes of Definition   **72**
Defining the Terms in Your Argument   **74**
Methods for Defining Terms   **77**
The Definition Essay   **82**
Writing an Essay of Definition   **82**

SAMPLE ANALYSIS

The Missing Element: Moral Courage
BARBARA TUCHMAN   **84**

A historian argues that the ills of American society stem from our leaders' failure to stand up for values that any educated person should know are worth standing up for.

READINGS FOR ANALYSIS

The Nature of Prejudice
GORDON ALLPORT   **92**

Identifying other people's prejudices is easy, observes a Harvard psychologist, but sometimes it takes careful definition to help us spot our own.

Saturday Night
SUSAN ORLEAN   **94**

A reporter roams the United States to discover what Saturday night means to Americans.

Everything a good restaurant ought to be [advertisement]   102

EXERCISES FOR REVIEW   **103**

4. ***Support***   **104**

Types of Support: Evidence and Appeals
    to Needs and Values   **104**
Evidence   **106**
Evaluation of Evidence   **112**
Appeals to Needs and Values   **120**
Evaluation of Appeals to Needs and Values   **126**

SAMPLE ANALYSIS

Lotto Is Financed by the Poor and Won by the States
PETER PASSELL   **127**

Legalized lotteries are a "cash cow" state governments have learned to love,
writes a *New York Times* reporter. But the data suggest that the public is being
milked.

READINGS FOR ANALYSIS

Economic and Social Impact of Immigrants
STEPHEN MOORE   **131**

The facts indicate that immigrants "do not just take jobs, but create jobs"
through their consumption and initiative.

Playing Favorites
PATRICIA KEEGAN   **135**

Men continue to outperform women academically, grants an educational
analyst — but not because of innate intellectual superiority.

Gas heat makes me nervous [advertisement]   **140**

EXERCISES FOR REVIEW   **141**

5. ***Warrants***   **142**

Types of Warrants   **148**
Evaluation of Warrants   **156**

SAMPLE ANALYSIS

The Case for Torture
MICHAEL LEVIN   **157**

A philosophy professor reasons that if torture is the only way to squeeze life-
saving information from a kidnapper or terrorist, we should overcome our
repugnance and apply the electrodes.

READINGS FOR ANALYSIS

A Proposal to Abolish Grading
PAUL GOODMAN   **161**

The author of *Growing Up Absurd* argues that if the goal of higher education *is* education, we should use tests that foster learning, not competition.

Here Comes the Groom
ANDREW SULLIVAN **164**

A graduate student explains why allowing gays and lesbians to marry is not a "radical step" but a fair and practical advance of existing laws.

Death Penalty's False Promise: An Eye for an Eye
ANNA QUINDLEN **169**

A columnist for the *New York Times* pits her gut response to a mass murder against her intellectual opposition to the death penalty.

Success has its own rewards [advertisement] **172**

EXERCISES FOR REVIEW **173**

6. Language and Thought **175**

The Power of Words **175**
Connotation **177**
Slanting **179**
Picturesque Language **182**
Concrete and Abstract Language **184**
Short Cuts **188**

SAMPLE ANALYSIS

Nox Quondam, Nox Futura!
RICHARD MITCHELL **196**

A well-known word watcher castigates academics who predict that society won't suffer if most of the population in the future is illiterate.

READINGS FOR ANALYSIS

The Speech the Graduates Didn't Hear
JACOB NEUSNER **200**

A scholar's caustic commentary on student-faculty relations indicts college as a ludicrously inappropriate preparation for the unforgiving world outside.

Erasing the "R" Words
HELEN E. AND R. LYNN SAULS **202**

Passages from textbooks of three different eras illustrate the claim of two college professors that religion has become a taboo subject in the classroom.

Good taste comes naturally to women all over New England [advertisement] **206**

EXERCISES FOR REVIEW **207**

7. *Induction, Deduction, and Logical Fallacies*   208

Induction   **209**

SAMPLE ANALYSIS

   The Silenced Majority
   BARBARA EHRENREICH   **211**

   A social critic worries that media messages reflect a "parochialism" of the professional middle class, who are cut off from the lives and struggles of the American majority.

Deduction   **214**

SAMPLE ANALYSIS

   Women Know How to Fight
   RUTH WESTHEIMER   **219**

   A psychologist argues that, as women in other countries are trained for and serve in combat, American women should have the right and the responsibility to do the same.

Common Fallacies   **223**

READINGS FOR ANALYSIS

   On Nation and Race
   ADOLF HITLER   **233**

   This excerpt from *Mein Kampf* expounds the principles of Nazi racist ideology.

   A Criminal Justifies Himself
   TONY PARKER and ROBERT ALLERTON   **239**

   "So violence is wrong. . . . But on a day-to-day level, it just happens that it's a tool of my trade." A career felon discusses the nature of his vocation.

   A trap can catch more than a mouse [advertisement]   **247**

EXERCISES FOR REVIEW   **248**

PART TWO

Writing and Researching Arguments   251

8. *Writing an Argumentative Paper*   253

Finding an Appropriate Topic   **254**
   Invention Strategies   254   Evaluating Possible Topics   254
   To This Point   256

Defining the Issues   **256**
> *Preparing an Initial Outline   256   Case Study: Coed Bathrooms   256*
Organizing the Material   **259**
> *Defending the Main Idea   260   Refuting the Opposing View   261*
> *Presenting the Stock Issues   261   Ordering Material*
> *for Emphasis   262   Considering Scope and Audience   262*
> *To This Point   264*
Writing   **264**
> *Beginning the Paper   264   Guidelines for Good Writing   267*
Revising   **270**
Preparing the Manuscript   **271**
Review Checklist for Argumentative Papers   **271**
A Short Student Argument   **272**

> ***The New Drinking Laws: A Sour Taste***
> *CLEO BOYD*   **273**

9.   *Researching an Argumentative Paper*   277

Getting Started   **277**
Mapping Research: A Sample Outline   **278**
Using Primary Sources   **279**
Using Secondary Sources: The Library   **280**
> *The Card Catalog and Catalog Access System   280   Encyclopedias*
> *282   Indexes   283   Abstracts   284*
Reading with a Purpose   **285**
> *Taking Notes   285   Quoting   288   Paraphrasing   289*
> *Summarizing   290   Avoiding Plagiarism   291   Keeping Research*
> *under Control   293   To This Point   293*
MLA System for Citing Publications   **294**
APA System for Citing Publications   **298**
A Sample Research Paper   **300**

> ***Why We Don't Need Zoos***
> *AMANDA REPP*   **301**

PART THREE

Opposing Viewpoints   311

10. *Abortion*   315

> ***Is Abortion Ever Equal to Murder?***
> *HOWARD H. HIATT and CYRUS LEVINTHAL*   **316**

A physician and a professor of biology propose that fetal brain development ought to be the guideline for determining when life begins.

Abortion Is Not a Civil Right
GREG KEATH   **318**

The president of Black Alliance for Family declares that African-Americans "cannot permit the public to continue to imagine that we are obediently following our national leaders in endorsing abortion on demand."

Nine Reasons Why Abortions Are Legal
PLANNED PARENTHOOD   **320**

An advertisement outlines why abortion should be legal and rebuts the claims of anti-abortion groups.

Public Shouldn't Pay
E. L. PATTULLO   **325**

A letter to the *New York Times* asks why, if abortion is a private matter, so many abortions are funded with public money.

Too Many Abortions
COMMONWEAL   **325**

A Catholic journal argues that abortion represents a failure of that "exercise of autonomy, self-esteem, and responsibility" so crucial to feminists.

Parents Also Have Rights
RONNIE GUNNERSON   **328**

A stepmother writes that if a pregnant teenager's parents are responsible for mother and child, they should have the right to decide whether the mother can keep her baby.

Abortion Consent Law Creates Support System
JULIET K. MOYNA   **331**

A college student reasons that a parental consent law would "force society to wrestle with the same responsibilities that it has been forcing women to handle alone since the birth of the sexual revolution."

Parental Consent Could Justify Forced Abortion
ANGELA R. HOLDER   **332**

A professor of pediatrics ponders the unreasonable powers a consent law would grant parents.

A Problem for Couples
ARTHUR B. SHOSTAK   **333**

A sociology professor urges state lawmakers to enact "legislation that is both pro-choice and pro-couple."

THINKING AND WRITING ABOUT ABORTION   **335**

11. AIDS Testing 336

Don't Tell Me on Friday
THOMAS RICHARDS **337**

An actor who tested positive for AIDS antibodies tells why he thinks taking the test is a positive step.

AIDS: In Plagues, Civil Rights Aren't the Issue
RICHARD RESTAK **339**

A neurologist writes, "To take a position that the AIDS virus must be eradicated is not to make judgments on morals or lifestyles. It is to say the AIDS virus has no 'civil rights.'"

How Not *to Control the AIDS Epidemic*
MATHILDE KRIM **343**

Surveying the history of AIDS, a leading researcher concludes that mandatory testing is "clearly *not* the way to attempt to control this epidemic."

HIV Testing: Voluntary, Mandatory, or Routine?
THERESA L. CRENSHAW **347**

A doctor systematically addresses the objections to required testing and anticipates a time when "being tested for AIDS will become a way of life."

AIDS: What Is to Be Done?
HARPER'S FORUM **355**

A symposium of experts engages in a wide-ranging debate on the dilemmas of AIDS testing.

Discrimination Goes On
ROBERT H. COHEN **360**

A letter to the *New York Times* asserts the need for a national commitment to end discrimination against those with AIDS; otherwise those who suspect they are infected will never come forward to be tested.

THINKING AND WRITING ABOUT AIDS TESTING **361**

12. Animal Rights 362

Animal Liberation
PETER SINGER **363**

Framing his case as a book review rather than as a partisan defense, a leading advocate of animal rights presents a chilling range of indictments of human "speciesism" and the suffering it inflicts on other living creatures.

Vivisection
C. S. LEWIS **375**

A Christian scholar reasons that if we dismiss the notion of "total difference between man and beast," it is inevitable that any argument for experimenting on animals can become an argument for experimenting on "inferior" men.

The Trials of Animals
CLEVELAND AMORY   **379**

Let the public witness the atrocities committed on animals behind closed laboratory doors, urges an animal-rights activist; experimenters have been judge and jury long enough.

Vigilant Protocol
THOMAS E. HAMM, JR.   **381**

A director at the Stanford University medical school details the stringent regulations his institution imposes on scientists before they are allowed to experiment upon animals.

Holding Human Health Hostage
MICHAEL E. DEBAKEY   **383**

Asserting that major medical breakthroughs are unthinkable without animal experimentation, a pioneering heart surgeon questions whether the right of the sick to relief is of less importance than "the right of abandoned animals to die in a pound."

Alternatives to Animals
THE ECONOMIST   **386**

This report balances the fiscal reasons for non-animal medical experimentation against the limits of its usefulness.

Animals and Sickness
THE WALL STREET JOURNAL   **389**

An editorial lambastes the tactics and "professional activists" of the animal-rights movement, "a clear and present danger to the health of us all."

Breakthroughs Don't Require Torture
STEPHEN ZAWISTOWSKI, SUZANNE E. ROY, STEPHEN KAUFMAN, and MARJORIE CRAMER   **391**

Readers take exception to the false claims and distortions they detect in the *Wall Street Journal* editorial.

In Defense of the Animals
MEG GREENFIELD   **393**

A *Newsweek* columnist takes a stand in "the muddled, middling, inconsistent place" where some uses of animals are okay, and some aren't.

THINKING AND WRITING ABOUT ANIMAL RIGHTS   **395**

13. Collegiate Sports Reform 397

Should College Athletes Be Paid Salaries?
GEORGE SAGE and JOHN DAVIS **398**

A phys-ed professor and an NCAA official debate whether college athletes should become paid entertainers or remain unsalaried members of the university family.

What Can Be Done?
TED GUP **400**

A *Time* magazine correspondent's eight-point program for reforming college sports subordinates the role of athletics to the traditional educational function of the university.

College Basketball: Issues and Answers
BILLY PACKER **401**

A basketball analyst for *CBS Sports* sums up why Proposition 48's formula for athletic eligibility based on standardized test scores is a successful innovation.

Proposal 42 Closes the Door on the Poor
ACEL MOORE **402**

A sports editor explains why an amendment to Proposition 48 which would withhold scholarships from academically unprepared student-athletes is a bad idea.

The Case in Favor of Proposition 42
FREDERICK P. WHIDDON **403**

The president of the University of Southern Albama believes that Proposition 42 would not, in the long run, close the door on the poor.

Only Two Ways to Free College Sport
IRA BERKOW **405**

Accept that big-time college sports programs are purely profit-making entertainment, says this sportswriter. Then accept that there are but two choices for sports reform available to colleges.

Fair Play for College Athletes: Racism and NCAA Rules
HERBERT I. LONDON **407**

A former scholar-athlete recommends that coaches who cry foul over Proposition 42 should ask themselves "why their humanitarianism doesn't result in anything but cruel disappointment for the dropout."

Prop 48 Makes Athletes Study
CLIFF SJOGREN **410**

Proposition 48 is a proven success, writes the man who drafted it — but Proposition 42 is misguided legislation that *won't* make a good thing even better.

The Myth of the Student-Athlete
SHANNON BROWNLEE with NANCY S. LINNON   **413**

U.S. News reports that "college sport has grown into an expensive circus, driven by an insatiable appetite for winning, and amateur athletes are getting neither the moral guidance nor the education they bargained for."

THINKING AND WRITING ABOUT COLLEGIATE SPORTS REFORM   **418**

14. Environmental Policy   419

Overview of the State of the Environment: Toward the Nineties
WILLIAM K. REILLY   **420**

An official of the Conservation Foundation traces the factors that have complicated, and will complicate, the establishment of a successful environmental policy.

Nature Under Glass
JAMES R. UDALL   **423**

An environmental reporter surveys the data that anticipate the effects of global warming, concluding that the planet's destiny is cradled in human hands.

Getting Warmer?
JANE S. SHAW and RICHARD L. STROUP   **427**

Two associates at a Montana think tank argue that untrammeled free-market progress can prevent present and future environmental problems.

Rethinking the Greenhouse
THE ECONOMIST   **432**

Although prophecies of a greenhouse-effect apocalypse are likely to fade, a benefit will be the adoption of policies "whose by-product will be a curb on greenhouse gases."

Hot Air in the Greenhouse Debate
GLENN T. WILSON   **435**

A business school professor gives six reasons why global warming "is much less of a problem than painted by extremists."

Staggering Cost Is Foreseen to Curb Warming of Earth
PETER PASSELL   **435**

A New York Times report charts the economic implications of controlling global warming.

Bottom-Line Thinking Won't Save Our Climate
PETER H. GLEICK   **440**

The director of a global environmental program claims that waiting until cost-benefit reports are all in means "waiting until climatic changes are upon us."

THINKING AND WRITING ABOUT ENVIRONMENTAL POLICY **441**

15. Euthanasia 443

Death by Choice: Who Should Decide?
DANIEL C. MAGUIRE **444**

According to a professor of ethics, though few of us would grant a doctor, a family, or a panel of experts the moral right to end someone else's existence, we can't decide the question *whether* without considering *who.*

In Defense of Voluntary Euthanasia
SIDNEY HOOK **449**

Having survived a life-threatening illness during which he asked to be allowed to die, a philosopher explains why he still believes that his request should have been honored.

Euthanasia Is Not the Answer
MATTHEW E. CONOLLY **452**

Stop trying to secure patients the right to die, begs a physician. Instead help them to live out their last days in the relative comfort of hospices.

Consequences of Imposing the Quality of Life Ethic
EILEEN DOYLE **456**

In the attempts of euthanasia proponents to substitute a "quality of life" ethic for a "right to life" ethic, a nurse perceives a covert attack on cherished American principles.

Active and Passive Euthanasia
JAMES RACHELS **459**

The American Medical Association has condemned "mercy killing" but has condoned allowing a terminally ill patient to die. A philosopher of ethics asks whether it is truly kinder to watch someone yield to a slow and painful death than to hasten the patient's inevitable end.

That Right Belongs Only to the State
MORTIMER OSTOW **464**

A doctor argues that, just as no member of our society is entitled to take a life by murder or suicide, so the burden of making life-or-death decisions in medical cases should not fall on individuals.

A Living Will
CONCERN FOR DYING **466**

A document from a pro-euthanasia organization directs that a seriously ill patient be permitted to die rather than be kept alive by "medications, artificial means, or 'heroic measures.'"

Not Everybody Wants to Sign a Living Will
FELICIA ACKERMAN   **468**

A philosophy professor decries the current tendency to perceive hopelessly ill people as blots on the lives of their long-suffering loved ones.

A Time to Die
THE ECONOMIST   **469**

We should think of life in biographical rather than biological terms: "When a person (or his relatives) can see that a biography is finished, it is not for doctors to write a painful extra chapter."

THINKING AND WRITING ABOUT EUTHANASIA   **471**

16. Freedom of Speech   472

In Praise of Censure
GARRY WILLS   **473**

A political analyst reviews recent free-speech controversies to develop his point that censoriousness, not censorship, is an effective response to objectionable materials.

Interim Policy on Discrimination and Discriminatory Conduct by Students in the University Environment
THE UNIVERSITY OF MICHIGAN   **478**

Should some speech be protected on campus and some not? Yes, said the University of Michigan, and provided guidelines and examples.

The Debate over Placing Limits on Racist Speech Must Not Ignore the Damage It Does to Its Victims
CHARLES R. LAWRENCE III   **482**

A professor of law at Stanford University explains why racist speech does not deserve the protection of the First Amendment.

How to Handle Hate on Campus
THE NEW YORK TIMES   **486**

A student's abuse of free speech at a public university requires careful handling, not summary expulsion of the student.

Free Speech on the Campus
NAT HENTOFF   **487**

A "journalistic custodian of the First Amendment" asks, "If students are going to be 'protected' from bad ideas, how are they going to learn to identify and cope with them?"

Flag-Saving
MELVIN L. WULF   **492**

A columnist in *The Nation* argues that "totemization of the flag is inconsistent with the concept of the First Amendment."

The Dynamics of Flag-Burning
JAMES M. WALL   **494**

An editor of *Christian Century* writes that if we recognize the uniquely symbolic status of the flag, then we recognize that protecting it does not violate the First Amendment.

Legislating the Imagination
JON PARELES   **497**

A music critic believes that well-intentioned efforts to warn consumers about potentially offensive music "is, in effect, an attempt to regulate the imagination."

Not Just a Few Prudes . . .
DAVID J. MELTZ   **500**

A doctor objects to Pareles's blanket condemnation of warning stickers. "Labeling contents is not censorship, no matter how you make it try to fit that Procrustean bed."

THINKING AND WRITING ABOUT FREEDOM OF SPEECH   **502**

17. Legalizing Drugs   503

Drugs
GORE VIDAL   **504**

A novelist contends that smoking marijuana or shooting heroin is the right of every citizen, should he or she choose to do it. Instead of putting our faith in government regulation, let's try trusting our own common sense.

Should Drugs Be Legalized?
WILLIAM J. BENNETT   **506**

The nation's "drug czar" excoriates those who believe that "enforcing drug laws imposes greater costs on society than do drugs themselves."

Thinking about Drug Legalization
JAMES OSTROWSKI   **511**

An attorney argues that though prohibition may decrease the use of illegal drugs, its negative consequences outweigh the beneficial effects of legalization.

We're Losing the Drug War because Prohibition Never Works
HODDING CARTER III **516**

A political commentator insists that drug prohibition "can't work, won't work, and has never worked." It will only undermine the criminal justice system and the integrity of government.

War on Drugs Falls through the Crack
GUY PIAZZA **518**

A letter notes that Carter's argument first goes astray when he equates alcohol abuse with hard drug abuse — and the fallacies don't stop there.

Legalize Drugs? Not on Your Life
CHARLES B. RANGEL **519**

A congressman dismisses arguments for legalization as "nonsensical talk." Americans must formulate a detailed national battle plan for the war on drugs and commit to it.

We Already Know the Folly of Decriminalized Drugs
ELIZABETH GESSNER **521**

Claiming that drug use underwent a "de facto decriminalization" two decades ago, a letter to the *New York Times* warns that we must try enforcing penalties for drug use "before we give up and turn our society into a drug bazaar."

We Can Control Drugs, but We Can't Ban Them
IRA GLASSER **523**

The director of the ACLU argues that generalizing about cocaine from its effects on pathological users is "like trying to infer the effects of alcohol at cocktail parties by looking only at skid-row alcoholics."

THINKING AND WRITING ABOUT LEGALIZING DRUGS **524**

18. Pornography **526**

Notes from a Free-Speech Junkie
SUSAN JACOBY **527**

A "First Amendment junkie" breaks ranks with those feminists who battle pornography yet defend other equally repellent forms of free expression.

Pornography: Anti-Female Propaganda
SUSAN BROWNMILLER **530**

This passage from the feminist classic *Against Our Will: Men, Women, and Rape* argues that pornography, far from freeing sensuality from "moralistic or parental inhibition," is a male invention that dehumanizes women and reduces the female to "an object of sexual access."

Sexual McCarthyism
HUGH HEFNER   534

The publisher of *Playboy* magazine detects in a government report on the hazards of pornography a pervasive reliance on "deception, innuendo, and outright lies."

The Bitter Harvest of Pornography
HAVEN BRADFORD GOW   539

An editor of *Police Times* cites data to support his contention that pornography "helps create a moral and social climate that is conducive to sexual abuse and exploitation."

Feminists Are Wrong about Pornography
AL GOLDSTEIN   540

A publisher of erotica assails feminists and fundamentalists for their "hysterical" opposition to pornography.

Pornography on the March
BETTY WEIN   542

An editor at Morality in the Media denounces pornography's ubiquitous encroachment on everyday life and urges her readers to take action against the flood of smut.

Pornography's Many Forms: Not All Bad
BARRY W. LYNN   546

A spokesman for the ACLU writes that we must not mount a moral crusade against representations of sexual fantasies until we weigh the positive uses of sexual images.

The Place of Pornography
JEAN BETHKE ELSHTAIN   548

What is the place of pornography? What is its function? Why is there so much of it today? A political scientist offers succinct answers to these questions.

Pornography Here and Abroad
ARYEH NEIER   549

The "astounding level" of sexual violence in countries where pornography is banned leads a civil libertarian to believe that pornography's role in sexual abuse is insignificant.

THINKING AND WRITING ABOUT PORNOGRAPHY   **550**

PART FOUR

Classic Arguments   553

From Crito
PLATO   555

Unjustly imprisoned in ancient Athens, the philosopher Socrates explains to an old friend why an individual is never justified in breaking the laws of a government, no matter how convinced he is that a law is wrong.

A Modest Proposal
JONATHAN SWIFT   560

An eighteenth-century satirist concocts a chilling, ironic solution to the problems of Irish poverty and overpopulation.

Civil Disobedience
HENRY DAVID THOREAU   569

The author of *Walden* explains why it is reasonable, and often imperative, to disobey laws that one believes to be unjust.

Declaration of Sentiments and Resolutions, Seneca Falls
ELIZABETH CADY STANTON   588

This manifesto by the women of the 1848 Seneca Falls Convention adapts the language and structure of the Declaration of Independence to emphasize that half of America still waited to be freed from the chains of tyranny.

Professions for Women
VIRGINIA WOOLF   593

A literary foremother of contemporary feminism argues in 1931 that two cultural obstacles prevent women from expressing themselves honestly as writers.

Politics and the English Language
GEORGE ORWELL   599

In this 1946 essay, the author of *Nineteen Eighty-Four* suggests why the hand that pens a stale metaphor should not be trusted with the reins of government.

Letter from Birmingham Jail
MARTIN LUTHER KING, JR.   611

In 1963, the imprisoned civil-rights leader argues that nonviolent victims of unjust laws have the right to break those laws so long as they use nonviolent tactics.

I Have a Dream
MARTIN LUTHER KING, JR.   626

This stirring exhortation to marchers at a 1963 civil-rights rally rings out like a church bell with rhythm, imagery, joy, hope, and deep conviction. Don't just read the words — listen to the music!